AMAZING HISTORY

BURIED TREASURE

JOHN MALAM

W
FRANKLIN WATTS

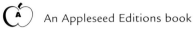
An Appleseed Editions book

First published in 2007 by Franklin Watts

Franklin Watts
338 Euston Road, London NW1 3BH

Franklin Watts Australia
Level 17/207 Kent St, Sydney, NSW 2000

© 2007 Appleseed Editions

Appleseed Editions Ltd
Well House, Friars Hill, Guestling, East Sussex TN35 4ET

Created by Q2A Media
Series Editor: Jean Coppendale
Designers: Diksha Khatri, Ashita Murgai
Picture Researchers: Lalit Dalal, Jyoti Sachdev
Illustrators: Hemant Arya, Adil A Siddiqui, Amir Khan

ISBN 978 0 7496 7537 0

Dewey classification: 622

All words in **bold** can be found in the glossary on page 30.

Website information is correct at time of going to press. However, the publishers cannot
accept liability for any information or links found on third-party websites.

A CIP catalogue for this book is available from the British Library.

Picture credits
t=top b=bottom c=centre l=left r=right m=middle
Cover images: Mel Fisher's Treasures Archives: b
Back cover: Julia Chernikova/ Shutterstock: tr
Scubabartek/ Dreamstime.com: 4b, REUTERS/ Ho New: 5b, Images&Stories, photographersdirect.com: 6br,
The Bridgeman Art Library: 7t, 18m, Mel Fisher's Treasures Archives: 8bl, 8br, www.hmsedinburgh.co.uk: 9t,
Imagestate Ltd/ Photlibrary: 10b, Library and Archives Canada: 11t, Julia Chernikova/ Shutterstock: 12t, Ron Watts/
Corbis: 13b, Q2A Media: 14b, 22b, Rich Bartell/ Shutterstock: 16t, The Trustees of the British Museum: 19t, 29b,
Vladimir Korostyshevskiy/ Shutterstock: 23t, Robert Harding Picture Library Ltd/ Photolibrary: 24b,
University of Pennsylvania: 26b, DHuss/ Istockphoto: 27b, Akivi33/ Dreamstime.com: 28b.

Printed in China

Franklin Watts is a division of Hachette Children's Books

Contents

What is buried treasure?

There is something magical about **treasure**. Under the ground, hidden in secret **tombs** and at the bottom of the sea, hidden treasure is waiting for people to find it.

Raiders of the past

Treasure-hunters have been hard at work all over the world for thousands of years. Wherever they have been, they have left tell-tale signs of their work. In Egypt, for example, the tombs of the ancient **pharaohs** (kings) are empty because long ago thieves broke in and stole their treasure. But they missed one amazing tomb and its treasure was found in our own time – see page 12.

Empty tomb

The pyramid of Pharaoh Khafre, built in about 2530 BC, was raided many years ago

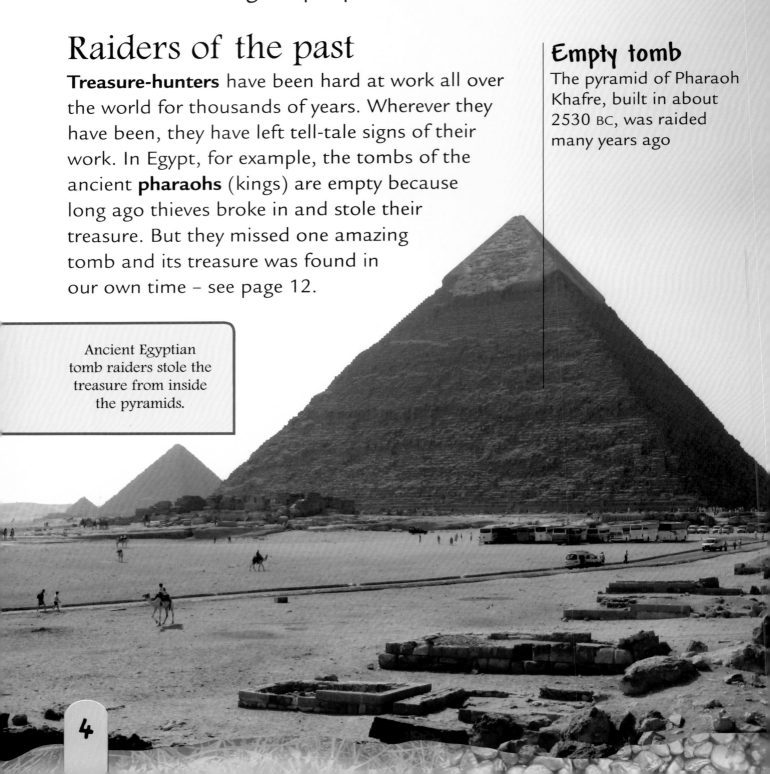

Ancient Egyptian tomb raiders stole the treasure from inside the pyramids.

Shipwreck treasure

The sea bed is littered with the wrecks of ships, and many sank taking their valuable cargoes with them. Ancient Greek and Roman ships were lost in the Mediterranean Sea. Then in the 16th century, heavily laden Spanish treasure ships sank as they sailed from South America to Europe. In the seas around China there are many wrecks laden with fragile **porcelain**. But shipwrecks hold more than just treasure – they are like time capsules, preserving a glimpse of what life was like on the day they sank.

HOTSPOTS

A ship called the Geldermalsen was smashed on a reef in 1752, on its way from China to Holland. Its cargo of thousands of pieces of Chinese porcelain fetched £10 million when it was sold in 1986.

Precious porcelain

Chinese dishes and bowls found on the wreck looking almost as good as new

Thousands of pieces of Chinese porcelain were lost when the *Royal Nanhai* sank over 400 years ago.

5

King's gold

Archaeologists have discovered many fabulous treasures. Some of these wonderful things may have belonged to ancient kings, which makes them even more precious.

Treasure of Troy

In 1873, the archaeologist Heinrich Schliemann found a stunning treasure in Turkey. He unearthed gold cups and headdresses, and silver objects that were 4,500 years old. Convinced he had found the ancient city of Troy, Schliemann called it Priam's Treasure, after a king of Troy. He smuggled the treasure to Germany, but it disappeared in 1945. It was found in 1993, in a museum in Russia.

Sophia Schliemann wearing gold jewellery discovered by her husband at Troy.

Archaeologists are still digging at Troy, revealing the ruins of ancient buildings.

Star symbol
This is the emblem
of the royal family
of King Philip II

This chest from the
royal tomb at Vergina
is made from 11 kg
of pure gold.

King Philip's chest of gold

As archaeologists dug away the soil of a huge
burial mound in Vergina, in northern Greece in
1977, they discovered a royal tomb. The tomb
was for King Philip II, father of Alexander the
Great. His body had been **cremated** (burned),
and his ashes placed inside a magnificent chest
of solid gold. The king had been buried with
his armour and weapons, and the walls of the
tomb were decorated with paintings. It was
just as it had been left, 2,300 years ago.

Treasure ships

Many a ship has ended its days as a wreck at the bottom of the sea, and some have gone to their watery graves loaded with valuable treasure.

Spanish gold

In 1622, the Spanish **galleon** *Atocha* sank off the coast of Florida, USA. The ship was sailing from South America to Spain loaded with a cargo of gold and silver bars, and 250,000 silver coins. The king of Spain ordered a search, but the *Atocha* was never found. However, Mel Fisher, an American treasure-hunter, eventually struck gold. In 1985, he located the wreck, and much of the treasure has been sold for millions of dollars.

NORTH AMERICA

Florida

Mexico

A diver holding a gold ingot he has just found from the wreck of the *Atocha*.

Gold bars
Some ingots measure 198 x 25mm

Gold and silver treasure from the *Atocha* treasure ship.

Well-armed
The ship carried 12 big guns, 8 machine guns and 6 x 533 mm torpedoes

Fast mover
HMS Edinburgh was a light cruiser and could reach a speed of 32 knots (59 km/h)

Torpedoed treasure

In 1942, the British warship *HMS Edinburgh* set sail from Russia with 465 bars of Russian gold. On the way to Britain the ship was torpedoed by a German submarine, and sank in the Barents Sea. It was not until 1981, in a daring **salvage operation**, that Keith Jessop, a British diver, recovered most of the gold from a depth of 245 metres. It was worth more than £43 million, and was shared between the British and Russian authorities, and the people who had paid for the expedition. Jessop's reward was £2 million.

HMS Edinburgh carried 93 wooden boxes loaded with bars of gold. In 1942, the gold was worth £1.5 million.

Barents Sea

Russia

Missing millions

Some buried treasure is still a mystery – no one really knows if it exists or not. Some people have spent years searching, but so far have failed to find it.

Alaric's treasure

In AD 410, Rome was attacked by an army from Germany led by Alaric. His soldiers are said to have gathered the city's treasure together before heading south through Italy. On the way, Alaric died. A legend says he was buried with the treasure in the bed of the River Busento in southern Italy, and then the river flowed over his grave. Some people think this is only a story, and there never was treasure... but this has not stopped treasure-hunters searching for it.

EUROPE

Italy

River Busento

Leaders of the ancient world were often buried with great wealth, so there may be some truth in the story of Alaric's burial.

Stolen riches
Alaric is buried, surrounded by treasure stolen from the city of Rome

Canada

Oak Island .

Hopeful treasure-hunters in 1931, beside the shaft of the Money Pit. A video taken inside the Money Pit in 1971 showed wooden chests, but the shaft collapsed before anyone could reach them.

HOTSPOTS

Alaric's soldiers used slaves to dig the bed of the River Busento and divert the water, so Alaric's body could be buried there. To make sure no one told where Alaric's tomb was, the soldiers killed all the slaves when their work was done.

The Money Pit

There's a fortune on Oak Island, Canada. Or is there? Treasure-hunters have wasted many years looking for it. Their shaft, more than 60 metres deep, is known as the Money Pit – not because it's full of treasure, but because digging it has cost them a lot of money! They have dug through layers of timber, the sides have collapsed and the shaft has flooded. But some still dream of finding treasure.

Egypt's treasures

When the pharaohs of ancient Egypt died, they were buried with everything they would need in the next life – and that included their most valuable and precious objects. Many people have dreamed of finding a pharaoh's tomb filled with treasure.

The gold funeral mask of Tutankhamun is decorated with priceless gems and coloured glass.

Wonderful things

Archaeologist Howard Carter peered into the tomb of ancient Egyptian pharaoh Tutankhamun in the Valley of the Kings, and said he could see 'wonderful things'. This was 1922, and Carter was about to uncover precious objects from 3,200 years ago. The greatest treasure was the pharaoh's gold mask, but there was also jewellery, a golden throne, a shrine and statues.

HOTSPOTS

Tutankhamun's tomb was broken into by tomb robbers before it was discovered by Howard Carter. But they seem to have been stopped before they could steal any of its treasure.

Golden mummies

Bahariya Oasis • Egypt • Valley of the Kings

In 1996, a donkey became stuck in a hole at the Bahariya Oasis, Egypt. Its owner climbed into the hole, and entered a tomb filled with 10,000 **mummies**. Many had masks covered in gold, and so the **cemetery** became known as the Valley of the Golden Mummies. Although they were not buried with the 'wonderful things' of a pharaoh, these mummies are among ancient Egypt's most amazing treasures.

The mummies seem to be arranged in family groups, with several generations buried together.

Ancient mummies

The mummies are about 2,000 years old

Pirate plunder

Imagine finding pirate treasure! Some people have, and the true stories of those who have spent years tracking it down are as exciting as the tales of the pirates themselves.

Black Sam's booty

In the early 1700s, the North American coast was terrorized by the pirate Sam Bellamy, also known as 'Black Sam'. In 1717, his ship, the *Whydah*, sank in a storm off Cape Cod, Massachusetts. Bellamy's loot of 180 bags of gold and silver coins vanished to the bottom of the sea. In 1984, Barry Clifford, an American treasure-hunter, located the *Whydah*, but only 15,000 coins have been found so far. Clifford is convinced he will find all of Bellamy's **booty**.

United States

Cape Cod

Cocos Islands

Gold jewellery found on the wreck of the *Whydah*.

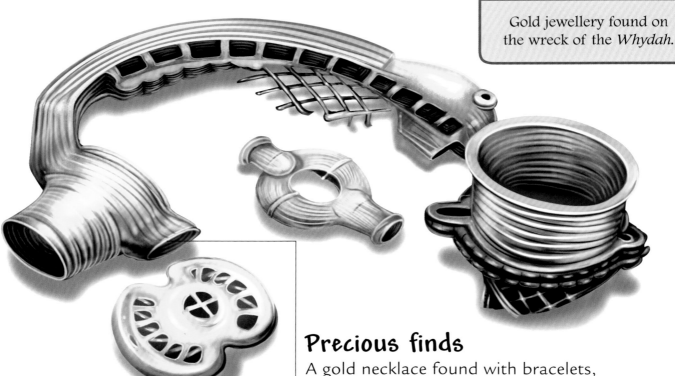

Precious finds
A gold necklace found with bracelets, knee and elbow decorations believed to have come from West Africa

Treasure island

In 1821, sailors on board the *Mary Dear* **mutinied** and stole the ship, which was on its way to Spain with a cargo of gold, silver and jewels. The crew murdered the soldiers guarding the cargo and sailed to the Cocos Islands in the Pacific Ocean. Most of the crew were eventually captured and executed. There is a legend that a map exists, showing where the sailors buried the treasure before they were arrested, but none has ever been found.

It is said that pirates buried their treasure for safekeeping. But most pirates died before they could reclaim it.

HOTSPOTS

The ship Queen Anne's Revenge *belonged to the fierce pirate, Blackbeard. It ran aground off the coast of North Carolina in 1718. The ship was discovered in 1996, and over 2,000 everyday objects have been found, but no treasure so far!*

Treasure chest

Pirate treasure is often said to be buried in chests

China's treasures

The amazing wealth of ancient China has come to light only recently, with fabulous discoveries of treasures buried long ago.

Each of the thousands of figures in the Terracotta army was armed according to his rank.

Clay soldiers
The life-size figures are made from terracotta, a type of pottery

Terracotta army

One of the most remarkable buried treasures was found in 1974, at Xi'an, in China. Archaeologists unearthed the tomb of the first Qin emperor and discovered more than 8,000 life-size figures of warriors and horses made from terracotta. The army of generals, soldiers, archers, cavalry and chariots was buried in pits to guard the emperor's tomb.

China

Xi'an •

Suits of jade

Long ago, important people in China were buried in suits of **jade** (a hard stone). The first jade burial suits were discovered in 1968, in the tomb of Prince Liu Sheng and his wife, Lady Dou Wan, who died 2,100 years ago. Their bodies were clothed from head to toe in jade squares sewn together with gold wire. Each suit was made from 2,500 pieces of jade, and more than 1 kilogram of gold.

HOTSPOTS

According to stories, Emperor Qin Shi Huang's tomb, 35 km east of Xi'an, contains booby-traps and a map of China with rivers of mercury!

Jade King

King Zhao Mo was buried in 122 BC

The jade suit of Zhao Mo, a king of early China. It is made from squares of green jade tied together with red silk.

Roman riches

In Roman Britain, valuables were buried by their owners if they had to flee enemies. Some people did not return, so the goods stayed hidden until found many years later.

The Mildenhall treasure

About 1,600 years ago, a rich Roman buried 34 silver dishes, bowls and spoons in Mildenhall, Suffolk. He never went back for them, and these valuable objects stayed in the ground until 1943, when a farmer dug them up by accident. The most stunning piece is the Great Dish, which is made from silver and measures 60 centimetres in diameter.

Great Britain

•• **Hoxne**
Mildenhall

The Great Dish from the Mildenhall treasure. Found in Britain, it was probably made in the eastern Mediterranean. It is one of the finest examples of Roman silver ever found.

Staring face
At the centre is Oceanus, god of the ocean

Dancing figures
Around the edge are dancing figures and creatures from Roman **mythology**

Gold and silver coins

In 1992, Eric Lawes was using a **metal detector** to search for a hammer in a field at Hoxne (say: hox-on), Suffolk. Instead of the lost hammer, his machine detected Roman treasure – 200 gold and silver objects and 14,780 coins! There were gold chains, finger rings and bracelets, a silver tigress, a pepper pot, bowls and spoons. Ten spoons had the name Aurelius Ursicinus on them – perhaps he was the original Roman owner.

HOTSPOTS

Both the Mildenhall treasure and the Hoxne treasure are on display at the British Museum, London, for everyone to see.

Heads up

Portraits of Roman emperors appear on the 'heads' side of the coins

Some of the thousands of gold and silver coins from the Hoxne treasure.

Lost ships

Finding a lost ship is an exciting way to discover treasure. One of the most famous ship's treasures of all time was found on dry land, not at the bottom of the sea.

Burial boat

One of England's first kings might have been buried in a boat. He was King Raedwald, who died in about AD 625. A boat found inside a mound at Sutton Hoo, Suffolk, in 1939, might be his grave. The boat and the body had rotted away, but his treasure was still there. Archaeologists found a warrior's helmet and weapons, gold coins from France and silver bowls from the Mediterranean.

Sweden

Great Britain

Stockholm Harbour

Sutton Hoo

Helmet
Reconstruction of the Sutton Hoo helmet

Buckle
Gold belt buckle from Sutton Hoo

The valuable objects found at Sutton Hoo suggest they belonged to a king.

Raising the Vasa

Carpenters, painters and sculptors spent years working on the **Vasa** warship, the pride of the Swedish navy. As it sailed out of the harbour on its first voyage in 1628, a light wind caught its sails. The ship leaned to the left, water rushed in through the **gun ports** and it sank. Divers recovered 53 of its 64 guns. The ship was then abandoned until 1961, when more than 15,000 objects were discovered. This was a treasure trove of everyday items used by sailors in the 17th century. Even a tub of butter was found!

The *Vasa* is the only warship from the 1600s to be seen anywhere in the world. The hull is covered in hundreds of sculptures.

HOTSPOTS

The wreck of the Vasa lay undisturbed just outside Stockholm Harbour for 333 years. No one really knows why the ship sank but historians think that the beautiful golden carvings were so heavy that they helped to unbalance the ship. When the gust of wind caught the sails, the Vasa just toppled over and sank.

Viking valuables

On their journeys to Europe, North Africa and the Middle East, the Vikings collected gold and silver. Sometimes they buried their treasure, and it is these **hoards** that excite us today.

Treasure chest

In 1840, workmen repairing the banks of the River Ribble, in Lancashire, found Europe's largest hoard of Viking age silver – 7,500 silver coins and 1,000 silver ingots and pieces of silver, weighing 40 kilograms, buried in a lead chest. Known as the Cuerdale hoard, it was buried by Vikings in about AD 905. Historians believe they may have been soldiers burying their treasure for safety.

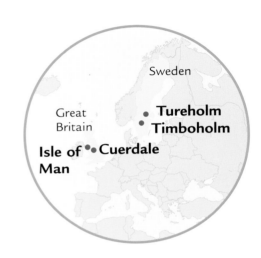

Silver coins and strips of twisted silver from the Viking age Cuerdale hoard.

Spirals
Over 20 golden spirals were found

Heavy hoard
The treasure weighed 7 kilos and included gold buckles, rings and ingots

Part of the treasure found at Timboholm. This is the largest hoard of gold discovered in Sweden so far.

Hundreds of hoards

Viking age gold jewellery was found at Tureholm, Sweden, in 1774. Sadly, most of it was melted down. In recent times, hoards have gone to museums, such as the gold ingots and **spirals** found in 1904 at Timboholm, Sweden. They belonged to a Viking goldsmith, who buried his raw material for safekeeping. The first Viking age hoard from the Netherlands was found in 1996, and in 2003 silver coins and ingots were found on the Isle of Man.

HOTSPOTS
Two amateur treasure-hunters out with their metal detectors in 2004, discovered a gold ring in a field in Wales. It had been lost by its owner in either the 9th or 10th century and had been buried ever since.

Wealth of South America

The lure of gold once drew treasure-hunters from Europe to South America. But the illegal work of modern-day raiders has done much to uncover the continent's buried treasure.

The legend of El Dorado

When the Spaniards first explored South America, they heard about a chief who covered himself in gold dust, then washed it off in a lake. From this came the legend of El Dorado (Spanish for 'the gilded one'). Treasure-hunters have searched for the golden kingdom, but all have returned empty-handed. However, there is some truth behind the legend. In Colombia, chiefs of the Muisca people really did coat themselves in gold dust before diving into Lake Guatavita.

Lake Guatavita
Colombia
Sipán
Peru

Treasure-hunters tried to drain Lake Guatavita by cutting a deep notch at the side of the lake.

Lord of Sipán

When **looters** dug into an ancient tomb at Sipán, Peru, they found gold objects made by the Moche people, 1,500 years ago. Archaeologists heard about the site, and in 1987 they discovered a tomb missed by the robbers. It was the tomb of a warrior priest, Lord of Sipán. Inside were feather headdresses, clothes, bead ornaments, gold jewellery and a fabulous gold headdress.

Lord Sipán's was the first intact royal tomb of the Moche people to have been found and studied.

Grave finds

Two male guards and three women were buried with the Lord of Sipán

25

Buried cities

Long ago, the rivers of Iraq changed course and cities became desert sands. In Italy, a volcano destroyed Roman towns. These disasters hid treasures for us to uncover today.

Royal cemetery of Ur

British archaeologist Leonard Woolley found some spectacular treasure at Ur, an ancient city in southern Iraq. In the 1920s, he found a cemetery with tombs of kings and queens, which was about 4,500 years old. The rulers were buried with priceless objects, including a golden ram caught in a bush, a king's gold helmet and a queen's gold headdress. A lyre (like a harp) and a decorated board for playing games on were among the many other treasures found in the **royal cemetery**.

Golden ram
The goat's fleece is made from shell, and its skin is gold leaf

Italy

Pompeii **Ur**
Iraq

The golden ram from Ur is one of the most famous finds from the ancient city. The ram may have been used to support a bowl.

City of ash

The volcano Vesuvius erupted in AD 79, and destroyed the Roman town of Pompeii, Italy. The town vanished beneath a deep layer of ash. The first **excavations** at Pompeii took place in the 1700s, and work there is still going on today. Building by building, street by street, the ruins are being uncovered, revealing a complete Roman town that is one of the greatest treasures of the ancient world.

Many of the houses in Pompeii had mosaics on the floor, such as this one of a guard dog.

The ancient Roman town of Pompeii, with the volcano Vesuvius in the background.

HOTSPOTS

Hoards of Roman treasure have been found in and around Pompeii. These were all lost on 24 August AD 79, the day Vesuvius blew its top.

Finding treasure today

It is everyone's dream to find treasure – and for some people this dream comes true. The discovery of treasure makes news headlines, but not always for the right reasons.

The lure of treasure

Some modern treasure-seekers steal from tombs, shipwrecks, buried cities and even museums. They break the law and many also damage precious historic places. But not all treasure-hunters are like this. Archaeologists discover treasure all the time and what they find does not have to be gold or silver to be valuable. Broken pots, pieces of bone and bits of buildings are their treasure, which they use to help them find out more about the past.

Archaeologists are careful to record everything they find. Here, an archaeologist is using a grid to help him make an accurate drawing of two pots buried inside a circle of stones.

Field of gold

In 1948, three hoards of gold **torcs** (rings worn around the neck) were found in a field at Snettisham, in the east of England. Two years later, more were found in the same field, and then, in 1990, a metal detector-user unearthed 50 more torcs, 70 rings and bracelets and some coins! The field of gold held even more surprises, because archaeologists then found another five hoards of gold, silver and bronze torcs. The Snettisham torcs are about 2,000 years old.

Great Britain

Snettisham

Some of the gold and silver torcs found at Snettisham in 1990.

Tangled torcs

The soil was removed from around the torcs before they were lifted from the ground

Glossary

archaeologist A person who studies the remains of the past.

booty Stolen goods.

burial mound A small hill made of soil, built over the burial place of a dead person.

cemetery A place where human or animal remains are buried.

cremate To burn a dead body to ashes.

excavation An archaeological site where earth is dug and removed in an organized way to discover information or treasure.

galleon A large sailing ship, favoured by Spain in the 15th and 16th centuries.

gun ports Openings in a ship through which the cannons are fired.

hoard A large quantity of items saved by their owner, often by burying in the ground.

ingot A rectangular block of metal, especially gold or silver.

jade A hard stone, usually green in colour, that is carved to make jewellery and other items.

looter A person who steals objects from an ancient site, in order to sell them.

metal detector A machine used to search for metal objects buried in the ground.

mummies The preserved bodies of dead people or animals.

mutiny A rebellion by sailors against their captain or commanding officers.

mythology A collection of stories or traditions that may mix up facts and fiction.

myrtle A flowering, evergreen shrub.

pharaoh A ruler or god-king of ancient Egypt.

porcelain A type of fine pottery, first made in China.

royal cemetery A place where kings, queens, and other members of a ruling family are buried.

salvage operation The recovery of cargo from the wreck of a ship, soon after it has sunk.

spirals Gold shaped into bracelets and rings.

tomb A place where a person is buried. It may (or may not) contain treasure.

torc A large metal ring, made from gold, silver or bronze, worn around the neck.

treasure An object, or objects, of great value.

treasure-hunter A person who searches for treasure. Some treasure-hunters damage ancient sites and break the law in their search for treasure (looters). Others work with archaeologists.

Index

Webfinder

http://ina.tamu.edu/ub_main.htm – the *Uluburun* shipwreck, one of the world's oldest wrecks

www.vocshipwrecks.nl/home_voyages3/geldermalsen.html – the *Geldermalsen* and its cargo of Chinese porcelain

www.vasamuseet.se/Home/Vasamuseet/Om.aspx – the *Vasa* shipwreck

www.archaeology.co.uk/ca/timeline/saxon/suttonhoo/ship/suttonhoo.htm – the Sutton Hoo treasure

www.mildenhallmuseum.co.uk/mildenhall_treasure.htm – the Mildenhall treasure

www.unmuseum.org/oakisl.htm – the Oak Island Money Pit